Steam in West Germany

Frontispiece. A pair of unrebuilt pacifics, Nos. 001 008-2 and 001 088-4 leaving Neuenmarkt-
Wirsberg on train E658, the 13.13 Hof-Bamberg-Wurzburg-Heidelberg-Saarbrucken combined
on this occasion with train D852, the 13.13 Hof-Bamberg-Nurenberg. The train was divided at
Bamberg and included through coaches from Gorlitz and Dresden in East Germany. 12 May
1973   *J. S. Whiteley*

Steam in West Germany

J. S. Whiteley
&
G. W. Morrison

Oxford Publishing Co. Oxford

ISBN 0 902888 72 2

Printed by B. H. Blackwell (Printing) Ltd.
in the City of Oxford.

Acknowledgement

The authors would like to thank all the photographers
who have so kindly contributed material and whose
assistance has we hope resulted in a balanced
selection of pictures.

Published by

Oxford Publishing Co.
8 The Roundway
Headington
Oxford.

INTRODUCTION

Since the demise of steam in Britain more and more interest has been shown in continental railways, particularly those of West Germany where steam locomotives have been retained in large numbers. This is because the German Federal Railway (Deutsche Bundesbahn) has adopted a policy very different to British Rail in maintaining an efficient fleet of steam locomotives pending completion of electrification which subsequently will release more modern diesels for secondary routes. Steam motive power will probably disappear, therefore, in 1977.

Few people will disagree that some of the German steam locomotives, although very different in appearance to the clean lines of British steam locomotives were equally impressive. British enthusiasts, therefore, have had almost another decade to enjoy sights like oil burning pacifics working heavy express passenger trains around Osnabruck and Rheine, the handsome Prussian engines working on particularly picturesque lines in the Black Forest area of Southern Germany and the last of the magnificent 01 pacifics working from the Bavarian town of Hof.

To understand the development of steam locomotives in West Germany we must go back to the period after the First World War. It was in 1920 when the railways of the eight States of pre-First World War Germany were unified and came to form the Deutsche Reichsbahn, subsequently coming under Government control in 1924. The Deutsche Reichsbahn which controlled the whole of the German railway system in this inter-war period is not to be confused with the post-Second World War East German railway which retained the name Reichsbahn after the country was split. The railway of the new German Federal Republic (West Germany) being known as the Deutsche Bundesbahn.

The Reichsbahn inherited a very mixed bag of not particularly significant nor useful locomotives, the exceptions being the standard designs of the Prussian State Railway, notably the P8 4-6-0 which survived for so long, together with the various goods counterparts and also the T18 4-6-4 tank locomotives and the T16 0-10-0 tank locomotives. After the 1923 depression the original Deutsche Reichsbahn was succeeded by a government-controlled system which was also called the Reichsbahn. The main intention of the new Reichsbahn was to introduce a new range of standard locomotives and by 1925 the Central Design Office had drawn up a totally new set of designs, many based on old Prussian ones, to cover all motive power requirements. Top priority was given to the introduction of a new pacific which emerged in 1925 in the form of a four-cylinder compound (Class 02), and a two-cylinder simple, (Class 01) which entered service the following year. The two designs were evaluated and it was decided to order only the two-cylinder simple pacific, construction commencing again towards the end of 1927. By 1938 231 of these pacifics had been built, the ten 02s were rebuilt as 01s between 1938 and 1942 and renumbered into the 01 series taking the total number of engines in this fine class to 241.

From 1925 onwards, under the standardisation plan, other classes which were built in large numbers included a heavy 2-10-0 freight locomotive (classes 43 and 44) and a very successful 2-8-2 tank locomotive (Class 86). In addition a light 2-6-0 (Class 24), its tank engine version, a 2-6-2T (Class 64) and several other classes were built in small numbers for specialised work.

During the 1930s a very fine 2-8-2 mixed traffic locomotive was introduced (Class 41), a lighter pacific (Class 03) and a lighter 2-10-0 freight locomotive (Class 50). It was on this class 50 that the Kriegsloks (war locomotives) of class 52 were based and these were built in vast numbers until the immediate post-war years.

The 01 pacifics were superseded in 1939 by a new three-cylinder simple, the 01^{10}, which was built in streamlined form together with the light-weight version, the 03^{10}. Construction of these machines was ended prematurely by the Second World War and they were eventually returned to service after the war minus their streamlining. They were subsequently rebuilt from 1953 with a larger high-performance boiler. Although construction of various classes continued after the war the only notable new introduction was a 2-6-2 mixed traffic locomotive (Class 23) and completion of No. 23 105 in December 1959 signified the end of steam locomotive construction for the Deutsche Bundesbahn.

Such then is the very brief history of the West German railway system in the days of steam. If the collection of photographs in this book gives half as much pleasure to our readers as we have derived from our railway trips to West Germany, then we shall be well satisfied.

J. S. Whiteley   G. W. Morrison
January, 1976.

Morning departure from Neuenmarkt-Wirsberg;
Unrebuilt pacific No. 001 173-4 built by Henschel
in 1936 leaves with the 06.40 semi-fast from Hof
to Frankfurt and Dortmund on 7 May 1973.
                                    J. S. Whiteley

Evening shadows fall on 01 pacific No. 001 202-1 as it prepares to leave Neuenmarkt-Wirsberg with a Wurzburg-Hof express. This locomotive was also built by Henschel, and although un-rebuilt has a modified front end. The locomotive depot can be seen in the background on the right hand side. 12 September 1969.

G. W. Morrison

Above left. The well illuminated front end of 4-6-0 No. 038 711-8 inside Freudenstadt shed on the evening of 11 May 1972.

J. S. Whiteley

Below left. Two of the 35 rebuilt Deutsche Reichsbahn 01s, 01-528 and 01-530 head for East Germany near Honebach at the summit of the climb out of Bebra, on the 09.37 Monchengladbach-Kassel-Leipzig express. 6 May 1973. *G. W. Morrison*

Above. A class 44 2-10-0 rumbles across the River Mosel at Eller with a rake of empties bound for Koblenz. 4 June 1969. *A. G. Orchard*

Above. A class 86 2-8-2T ambles along the picturesque branch from Neumarkt to Beilngries on the morning of 13 May 1972. It was one of a large class of tank engines built between 1928 and 1943 for the Deutsche Reichsbahn.　*R. J. Manton*

Above right. 2-6-2 No. 023 058-1 pauses at Sulzdorf, near Schwabisch Hall on the Sunday 16.06 Crailsheim-Heilbronn. 10 September 1972. These mixed traffic engines were intended as replacements for the 38s (Prussian P8s) but only 105 were built from 1950 until construction of steam locomotives for the Deutsche Bundesbahn ceased in 1959.

J. S. Whiteley

Below right. 4-6-2 No. 001 073-6 built in 1928 accelerates away from Cochem with a morning semi-fast from Saarbrucken to Koblenz. On the right a three-cylinder 2-10-0 No. 044 674-0 waits for the road with a train of empties. 10 September 1970.

J. S. Whiteley

Above. A nocturnal picture of an oil-burning Class 42 at Rheine. 4 April 1971.   *L. A. Nixon*

Above right. 012 068-3 arriving at Lingen on the lunchtime express to Rheine and Munster.   *M. Welch*

Below right. Two class 94s on shed at Wuppertal on 24 March 1968.
                                    M. Welch

Above left. 4-6-2 No. 001 111-4 restarting the 07.06 stopping train from Hof to Lichtenfels on 12 May 1973. This particular locomotive was built by Schwartzkopff in 1934 and by the end of 1938 231 01s had been built by six different firms. Subsequently ten class 02 pacifics were rebuilt as 01s and renumbered into the 01 series bringing the total number of engines in this fine class to 241. *J. S. Whiteley*

Below left. Three cylinder 2 10 0 No. 44 014 receives banking assistance on a mammoth freight consisting of some empty coaching stock on the climb from Paderborn to Altenbeken. The type 44 was the standard heavy freight engine of the Reichsbahn and Bundesbahn with almost 2,000 being built between 1926 and 1949.

D. Gouldthorp

Above. Rebuilt oil fired Class 41 No. 41 169 climbs out of Osnabruck with a northbound freight for Bremen. Several of the original class of 366 41s, were rebuilt with larger welded boilers and in some cases new cylinders, and roller-bearing big and little ends. The locomotives which were rebuilt as oil burners were later re-classified 042s, to conform with the D.B. computerised numbering system. 21 September 1968. *G. W. Morrison*

Above. On a wet May afternoon a class 38 4-6-0 heads the 16.15 Hausach-Freudenstadt near Alpirsbach.

J. S. Whiteley

Below. Two unrebuilt 01s emerge from the pine woods near Marktschorgast on the 12.02 Ludwigshafen-Wurzburg-Bamberg-Hof on 12 May 1973.

J. R. P. Hunt

Above. 0-10-OT No. 094 538-6 leaving
Eibelshausen on a train from Ewersbach to
Dillenberg and Gonnern. 21 April 1971. *J. S. Whiteley*

Below. A class 44 crossing Altenbeken viaduct on a
mixed freight from Paderborn.   *D. Gouldthorp*

Above. 2-10-0 No. 052 186-8 pilots a class 50 2-10-0 on the climb from Hartmanshof to Neukirchen with a freight from Nurenberg to Weiden. 12 May 1973.   *J. S. Whiteley*

Above right. Oil-burning pacific No. 01 1074 climbing out of Osnabruck towards Bremen on the Holland-Scandanavia express. 2 June 1968.   *L. A. Nixon*

Below right. Lightweight two-cylinder pacific No. 03 014 climbing Junkerath bank with the 11-32 Saarbrucken-Cologne. These engines emerged in 1930 as a smaller and lighter version of class 01, the first 123 having a maximum axle-load of 17 tons and the remainder in a class of 298 having it increased to 18 tons.   *D. Gouldthorp*

Left. Perhaps the most handsome of the old Prussian designs, the class 78 (Prussian T18). It was a 4-6-4T being the tank engine version of the class 38 (Prussian P8) and over 500 were built between 1912 and 1924. Here No. 078 192-2 pauses at Aistaig on an afternoon Rottweil-Horb stopping train. 22 April 1971.

J. S. Whiteley

Above. Rebuilt pacific No. 001 131-2 nearing the summit of the notorious five mile climb at 1 in 40 from Neuenmarkt-Wirsberg to Marktschorgast (the Schiefe Ebene) on the 06.04 Wurzburg-Hof. This locomotive was built in 1935 by Henschel and re-boilered in 1966 with the boiler of 01 122 which had been rebuilt in 1958 but withdrawn from service after being involved in an accident in 1965. These rebuilt 01s were easily distinguished from their un-rebuilt counterparts having a boiler 4 inches greater in diameter at the front end, a shorter large diameter chimney and the steam and water feed pipes running over the top of the smokebox.

J. R. P. Hunt

Above. 2-10-0 No. 050 954-7 pilots a class 44 2-10-0 on a heavy southbound coal train crossing the River Mosel at Eller. 6 April 1971.   *L. A. Nixon*

Above right. 042 364-0 rests at Rheine during the night of 4 April 1971.
                                    L. A. Nixon

Below right. One of the few remaining active class 78s in 1970, No. 078 246-6 in the woods near Lauffen heading the 16.44 Rottweil-Villingen. 23 May 1970.
                                    G. W. Morrison

Above left. The class 65 was a heavy two-cylinder 2-8-4T introduced in 1951. Although it was a successful design only 18 were built, further construction ceasing in the mid fifties as dieselisation and electrification became more advanced. Here No. 065 008-5 hurries along with an early morning train from Darmstadt to Erbach. 2 September 1969.

L. A. Nixon

Below left. 64 049 on station pilot duties at Aalen. 4 June 1968.

L. A. Nixon

Above. Surely one of the most photographed viaducts in West Germany. A three-cylinder class 44 2-10-0 crossing Altenbeken viaduct on a freight from Paderborn.   *D. Gouldthorp*

Above. 065 018-4 near Ober Ramstadt on the 18.50 Darmstadt-Erbach train. 29 May 1969. *L. A. Nixon*

Below. The last regular passenger workings of the Prussian T16 0-10-0Ts were on the Dillenburg-Gonnern-Biedenkopf trains. No. 094 538-6 is seen not far from Dillenburg on the 14.42 to Gonnern. 21 April 1971. *G. W. Morrison*

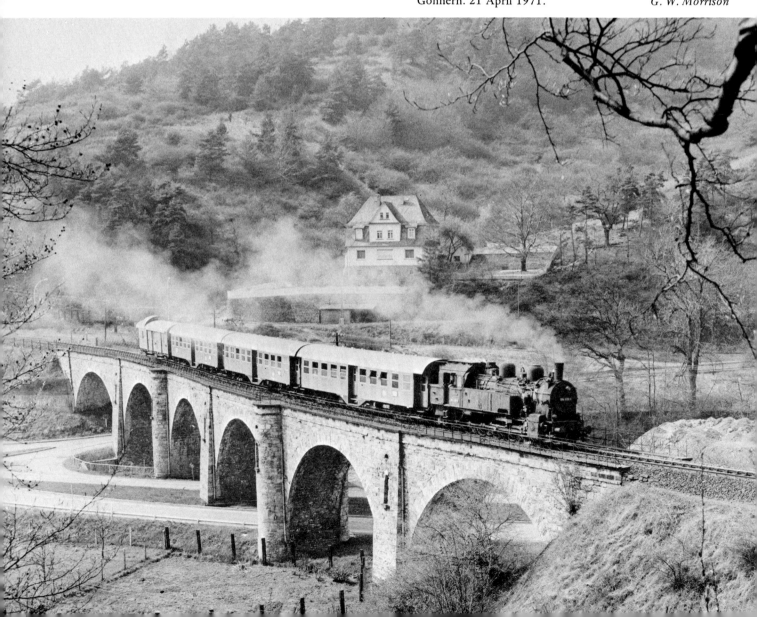

Above. A class 50 2-10-0 No. 051 679-9 passes Dillingen shed with a train of empty ore wagons. 22 May 1970.   *G. W. Morrison*

Below. The class 86 2-8-2 tank locomotives were built in large numbers by the Reichsbahn between 1928 and 1943. Here a member of the class simmers quietly on the evening of 10 May 1973 at Hof shed.   *J. S. Whiteley*

Above. After the Second World War the Deutsche Reichsbahn acquired seventy 01 pacifics. Thirty-five were subsequently rebuilt between 1961 and 1965 and were reclassified 01^5. These locomotives look totally different to their un-rebuilt counterparts having a newly designed boiler and semi-streamlined casing along the top. No. 01 0507-2 was one of eight rebuilt locomotives to be fitted with Box-Pok type driving wheels and is seen here climbing away from Bebra with the 11.42 Frankfurt (Main)-Leipzig-Frankfurt (Oder). 6 May 1973.   J. S. Whiteley

Above right. One of the ninety-two three-cylinder 03^{10}s which were originally streamlined. Twenty-six were rebuilt by the D.B. between 1956 and 1958, one of which was No. 03 1043 which is seen at Kassel having arrived on a local train. These rebuilds had slightly smaller boilers than those used for the rebuilt 01^{10}s. 12 September 1966.
G. W. Morrison

Below right. The three-cylinder 2-8-2 class 39 (Prussian P10) was a powerful mixed traffic locomotive Here No. 39 230 is seen at Friedrichshafen on the 16.58 to Radolfzell on 2 June 1965.
Brian Stephenson

Above left. An un-rebuilt 01 pilots a rebuilt 01 away from Neuenmarkt-Wirsberg on the combined 13.13 Hof-Saarbrucken and 13.13 Hof-Nurenberg which was divided at Bamberg. 7 May 1973.   *J. S. Whiteley*

Below left. Two-cylinder 2-6-2 No. 023 028-4 pulling away from Goldshofe with the 10.14 Crailsheim-Ulm. 11 September 1972.   *J. S. Whiteley*

Above: 4-6-0 No. 038 509-6 tackles the steep climb (believed to be 1 in 45) from Lautlingen to Ebingen with train 4318, the 12.18 Tubingen-Sigmaringen on 1 April 1970.   *Brian Stephenson*

Class 50 2-10-0 No. 050 361-5 piloting class 44 2-10-0 No. 044
482-8 emerge from the Petersberg tunnel and cross the River
Mosel at Eller on a northbound train of empty hoppers. The class
50 was a much lighter locomotive than the class 44 having an
axleload of only 15½ tons compared to 19¾ tons of the class 44.

L. A. Nixon

Class 38 4-6-0 No. 038 650-8 suitably decorated at
the front on the occasion of its last day in service.
It is seen here shunting its last train at Horb after
arrival from Rottweil whilst another 38 arrives tender
first with the stock of the 18.38 train to Freudenstadt.
It had rained all day but fortunately the sky cleared
miraculously just in time to get one photograph of
her in the late afternoon sun before the locomotive
went on shed for the last time. 12 May 1972.

J. S. Whiteley

Left. A class 44 2-10-0 No. 044 086-7 runs alongside the River Mosel between Neef and Bullay with a Koblenz-Trier express freight. 10 June 1971.

Michaeles Stephenson

Below. No. 078 410-8 on the turntable at Rottweil motive power depot. *J. Marsh*

Right. 2-10-0 No. 052 844-8 approaching Ravensburg on a northbound freight from Friedrichshafen. 12 September 1970.   *M. Welch*

Below. The first of the eighteen class 65s in mint condition near Ober Ramstadt on the 17.27 Darmstadt-Erbach. 29 May 1969.   *L. A. Nixon*

Left. Class 38 4-6-0 No. 038 650-8 leaving
Freudenstadt with train E1949, the 10.16
to Stuttgart which it worked as far as
Eutingen. 3 September 1971.
Michaeles Stephenson

Above. The three-cylinder class 44 2-10-0s
were extremely powerful locomotives and
although having a very large grate, most were
hand-fired. The fireman was obviously hard at
work on No. 044 463-8, seen here on a heavy
freight near Eptendorf heading for Rottweil.
24 May 1970.   *G. W. Morrison*

Above. Deep in the Black Forest something stirred; a class 38 4-6-0 pounds up the gradient towards Lossburg on the long climb from Alpirsbach heading the 09.11 Hausach-Freudenstadt on 22 April 1971.
J. S. Whiteley

Below. The class 43s were the oil burning equivalent of the class 44 2-10-0s and one is seen here passing Meppen on a southbound ore train. 17 October 1973.
M. Welch

Above. 001 168-4 nears Marktschorgast on the 17.09 Lichtenfels-Hof just as the sun re-appears after a heavy downpour. 11 May 1973.   *J. S. Whiteley*

Below. Lightweight pacific No. 003 168-2 leaving Ravensburg on the Saturdays only Ulm-Friedrichshafen. 12 September 1970.   *M. Welch*

Left. 18 601 was one of several four-cylinder compound Maffei pacifics rebuilt between 1953 and 1956 with a larger, all-welded boiler and it is seen here on the turntable at Ulm shed on 9 May 1959. One hundred and fifty nine of these locomotives were built between 1908 and 1930, initially for the Bavarian State Railway as class S3/6 and finally for the Deutsche Reichsbahn.
R. Shenton

Right. The Black Forest area could be very wet and 12 May 1972 was one such day. A class 38 4-6-0 runs alongside the River Kinsig between Wolfach and Schiltach with the 16.15 Hausach-Freudenstadt.
J. S. Whiteley

Left. 044 463-8 restarts a heavy freight from the loop at Fishingen after allowing an afternoon train from Rottweil-Horb to cross. 31 August 1970.
J. S. Whiteley

Right. A class 44 drifts into Cochem in the Mosel valley with a freight bound for Trier.
E. Bobrowski

Above left. A class 86 alongside an unserviceable 01 at Hof shed. 10 May 1973.

J. S. Whiteley

Below left. One of the old Prussian P8s No. 38 3603, built in vast numbers between 1906 and 1924 enters Kassel whilst a modern D.B. class 23 No. 23 013 waits to depart on a local train. 12 September 1966. *G. W. Morrison*

Above. 2-10-0 No. 044 388-7 climbs away from the Bamberg line at Oberkotzau and takes the route to Marktredwitz and Regensburg with a southbound freight from Hof.

E. Bobrowski

Above. Un-rebuilt class 01 No. 001 150-2 restarts the 16.40 Lichtenfels-Hof from Burgkunstadt on 5 April 1970.   *Michaeles Stephenson*

Above right. P8 No. 38 3559 heads the 14.58 Horb-Tuttlingen near Balgheim, south of Rottweil. 5 June 1968.   *L. A. Nixon*

Below right. 03 074 leaves Duren with an Aachen-Cologne stopping train.   *F. J. Bullock*

Above left. Rebuilt 01 No. 001 180-9 climbs the 1 in 40 of the Schiefe Ebene on train D853, the 11.06 Nurenberg-Bamberg-Hof. 11 May 1973.

J. S. Whiteley

Below left. One of the two oil burning three-cylinder class 10 pacifics, No. 10 001 enters Kassel with a train from Frankfurt and Giessen. These locomotives were built by Krupp for the Bundesbahn as late as 1957 and initially 10 001 burned coal but had auxiliary oil firing for heavy trains. It was later converted to burn only oil becoming identical to sister engine No. 10 002 which was constructed as an oil burner. These locomotives represented the ultimate development of the express steam locomotive in Europe. 12 September 1966.

G. W. Morrison

Above. 044 367-1 bursts out of the Petersberg tunnel as it approaches Eller with a Trier-Koblenz freight. 8 April 1971.

L. A. Nixon

Above left. A class 23 2-6-2 crosses the River Mosel at Bullay heading the 16.15 Cologne-Trier. 21 August 1964.

Brian Stephenson

Below left. Class 38 No. 038 553-4 emerges from a short tunnel on the particularly photogenic stretch of line between Schiltach and Alpirsbach heading the 09.11 Hausach-Freudenstadt. *J. S. Whiteley*

Above. Class 64 2-6-2T No. 064 109-2 leaves Worth with train 2335 the 13.34 Miltenberg-Aschaffenburg on 6 April 1970. These useful tank engines had an axle-load of 15 tons and five hundred and twenty were built between 1928 and 1940.

Michaeles Stephenson

Above. Un-rebuilt pacific No. 01 202 departs from
Marktredwitz on 21 May 1967 with train D141 the
14.42 Munich-Hof.   *Brian Stephenson*

Right. A class 44 crosses Neuenbeken viaduct on a
mixed freight.   *D. Gouldthorp*

Above. Oil burning pacific No. 01 1055 storms past Ostercappeln towards the summit at Vehrte en route to Osnabruck with a Westerland-Cologne express.   *G. W. Morrison*

Below. 001 150-2 working from Ehrang depot crosses the River Mosel at Eller heading train E1867, the 14.45 semi-fast from Trier to Koblenz. 6 April 1971.   *L. A. Nixon*

Above. 051 559-3 rests at Tubingen motive power depot in the early hours of 22 April 1971.

J. S. Whiteley

Below. An unidentified class 44 rumbles across the River Mosel at Eller on a southbound freight and disturbs the peace of a still April morning in 1971.

L. A. Nixon

4-6-2 No. 01 1055 storms out of Osnabruck heading the Holland - Scandinavian express. This locomotive was one of the fifty five streamlined 01^{10}s built from 1939 onwards which were rebuilt from 1953, most of them being converted to oil-burners. These oil burning locomotives were subsequently re-classified 012s under the D.Bs computerised numbering system. 23 September 1968.

G. W. Morrison

Above. Oil burning 2-10-0 No. 043 326-8 heading south from Meppen towards Rheine with an ore train from Emden. *D. Mills*

Below. A birds-eye view of the turntable and roundhouse at Rottweil with the traverser and straight road shed at the top left of the picture. *J. Marsh*

Above. Class 38 4-6-0 No. 038 711-8
slowing for the stop at Schenkenzell on
an all stations train from Hausach to
Freudenstadt and Horb. 6 August 1973.
J. S. Whiteley

Left. One of the eighteen class 65 2-8-4Ts
introduced in 1951, No. 065 013-5,
approaches Ober Ramstadt on an Erbach
to Darmstadt train. 25 September 1970.
G. W. Morrison

Above. Coal fired 2-10-0 No. 044 463-8, not long out of works, passes Altoberndorf with a freight bound for Rottweil. 22 April 1971.   *J. S. Whiteley*

Below. Oil-burning pacific No. 01 1060 passes through the woods near Ostercappeln en route to Osnabruck. 2 June 1968.   *L. A. Nixon*

Above. 01 Pacific No. 001 211-2 was built by Krupp in 1937 and rebuilt with larger boiler in 1959. It is seen here working hard on a 1 in 40 gradient near Marktschorgast on the 06.04 Wurzburg-Hof and receiving banking assistance in the shape of a V60 diesel.

E. Bobrowski

Above right. Class 50 2-10-0 No. 050 202-1 pilots class 38 4-6-0 No. 038 039-4 on a morning train from Rottweil to Horb. The 2-10-0 was required at Horb to bring a freight back to Rottweil and is piloting the 4-6-0 to avoid unnecessary light engine working. They are seen slowing for the stop at Eptendorf. 22 April 1971.

J. S. Whiteley

Below right. 01 1068 climbing out of Osnabruck heading an express for Hamburg on 2 June 1968. These rebuilt pacifics were fitted with new all-welded boilers but the bar frames of the locomotives were left untouched. These rebuilt oil burners were extremely economical from a maintenance point of view and their availability was increased enormously making them a very successful express passenger locomotive.

L. A. Nixon

Above left. Number comparisons at Aalen; 78 355, having arrived on a train from Ulm, runs light engine past 078 062-7 waiting to depart on the 17.11 local train to Schorndorf. 4 June 1968.   *L. A. Nixon*

Below left. Oil burning Deutsche Reichsbahn rebuilt 01⁵ working hard on the heavy 11.42 Frankfurt (Main)-Leipzig-Frankfurt (Oder). It is seen here nearing the summit of the climb out of Bebra at Honebach, just before crossing into East Germany. This picture was taken in May 1973 and at this time all the freight crossing into West Germany from the East were diesel hauled but the passenger trains were in the hands of these East German pacifics. These locomotives worked from Erfurt and were serviced at Bebra on arrival but never stabled overnight at Bebra.   *J. S. Whiteley*

Above. Early morning at Neuenmarkt-Wirsberg; On the left is a class 50 which has arrived with train 2808, the 05.30 stopping train from Hof to Lichtenfels. It is about to be overtaken by 01 pacific No. 001 008-2 on the right which is ready to leave with train E1886, the 05.51 semi-fast from Hof to Wurzburg. 7 May 1973.   *J. S. Whiteley*

Right. 044 463-8 wheels along a mixed freight past Talhausen.   *J. S. Whiteley*

Below. Three different variations of the class 50 2-10-0 at Osnabruck on 10 September 1966. No. 50 432 being the standard design, No. 50 2399 fitted with a Henschel mixing type feed-water heater and No. 50 4005 one of thirty-one fitted with a franco-crosti boiler.   *G. W. Morrison*

Above. 086 201-1 being watered at Beilngries after arriving on the 07.54 from Neumarkt. 13 May 1972.
J. S. Whiteley

Left. Crossing the "iron curtain"; Erfurt pacific No. 01 0530-4 nears Honebach on a Frankfurt (Oder)-Leipzig-Monchengladbach train on 14 May 1972. The photographer was standing on West German soil but the locomotive is actually still in East Germany, the lighter ballast incorporating some type of electric warning device and denoting the actual border. This is a most eerie location and not one to be recommended. A double barbed-wire fencing strikes off at right angles to the track and this is patrolled by heavily armed guards with guard dogs. There are intermittent sentry posts and not a blade of grass is allowed to grow near the East German side of the border which is protected by a mine field. Just behind the locomotive in the trees there is a pill box manned night and day and armed with high velocity machine guns.
J. S. Whiteley

Above. 2-10-0 No. 44 1118 crossing the River Mosel at
Bullay.
                                        D. Gouldthorp

Below. Lauda motive power depot on 21 April 1975.   *P. Thomas*

Above. A class 65 2-8-4T silhouetted near Ober
Ramstadt at dawn.　　　　　　*L. A. Nixon*

Below. 078 192-2 slowing for Dettingen on the 16.14 Rottweil-Horb.
　　　　　　J. S. Whiteley

Class 44 2-10-0 No. 44 332 passing Fishingen on a southbound mixed freight on 7 June 1968. These 2-10-0s had a tractive effort of 60,360lb making them the most powerful locomotives of the Deutsche Bundesbahn and amongst the most powerful in Western Europe. They were coal-fired and although a few locomotives were fitted with mechanical stokers this was rather surprisingly never adopted on a large scale by the D.B.

L. A. Nixon

Above. A heavy freight bound for Bremen approaches the summit of the climb out of Osnabruck at Vehrte headed by 2-10-0 No. 44 079. 21 September 1968.

G. W. Morrison

Right. Oil fired class 41 No. 41 166 pauses on Osnabruck Hauptbahnhof shed. On the right emerging from inside the shed is the rear of the oil carrying tender fitted to sister engine No. 41 168. 10 September 1966. *G. W. Morrison*

044 523-9 approaches Punderich heading a Koblenz-
Trier freight. 7 April 1970.   *Brian Stephenson*

Above. Two 38s resting overnight at Horb.
J. S. Whiteley

Below. 38 3551 with a semi-elliptical tender from a scrapped kriegslok drifts through the Black Forest on a Rottweil-Horb stopping train. 5 July 1968.
G. W. Morrison

Above left. Oil fired 01 pacific No. 01 1060 storms the last kilometre of the climb to Vehrte on a Hamburg-Cologne express. 11 September 1966.

G. W. Morrison

Below left. 78 298 arriving at Aalen on the 05.58 from Schorndorf. 4 June 1968.
L. A. Nixon

Above. Early Spring is probably the busiest time in the vineyards of the Mosel valley. Cultivation and preparation of the vineyards seems well advanced in this picture of a class 44 2-10-0 leaving the Petersberg tunnel at Neef en route for Trier with a freight from Koblenz. 6 April 1971.
E. Bobrowski

Above. 023 035-9 leaves the attractive town of Schwabisch Hall with the 14.35 to Heilbronn. 5 June 1971.

Brian Stephenson

Left. The nostrils of a rebuilt class 01^{10} pacific. These rebuilt locomotives retained their single blast-pipes and in this picture the arrangement of the exhaust outlets from auxiliaries can be clearly seen in the perimeter of the large diameter chimney.

J. W. Holroyd

050 596-6 restarts a mixed freight bound for Hof from Neuenmarkt-Wirsberg at the foot of the l in 40 climb to Marktschorgast. This locomotive is one of many fitted with a tender incorporating a guard's hut which made a guard's van on fitted stock unnecessary. 11 May 1973.
J. S. Whiteley

Above left. An 012 at rest;
No. 012 058-4 is seen at Rheine
shed between duties.

J. C. Miller

Below Left. An 012 in action;
No. 012 101-2 accelerates a
southbound semi-fast from
Lingen. The works can be
seen on the right of the
picture. *M. Welch*

Above. Un-rebuilt 01 pacific No. 001 150-2 with
the help of a V100 at the rear at grips with the
1 in 40 climb to Marktschorgast heading train
E659, the 07.51 Saarbrucken-Heidelberg-
Wurzburg-Hof, The Frankenland.
Although a very scenic stretch of line, northbound
trains were rather difficult to photograph because
of the thickly wooded sections and the sun being
predominantly on the wrong side of the train. This
in fact was the only train which could be
photographed at this location with the sun on the
correct side. 12 May 1973.

J. R. P. Hunt

Above. 2-6-2T No. 64 415 leaving Aalen on a train for Schorndorf. 7 July 1968.   *G. W. Morrison*

Below. Class 03 4-6-2 No. 03 089 speeds past Eller with the 10.25 Luxemburg to Koblenz train. 21 August 1964.

Brian Stephenson

Above. 044 178-2 heads the Ford car train past the neatly laid out vineyards of the Mosel on a particularly warm but hazy day in April 1971.
J. S. Whiteley

Below. 001 168-4 nears Hof Hauptbahnhof, having just passed Hof-Moschendorf with a train from Bamberg. 29 May 1969.
Brian Stephenson

A three-cylinder class 44 crosses the Mosel at Eller with
a freight from Koblenz to Trier. 6 April 1971.

E. Bobrowski

Un-rebuilt 01 No. 001 111-4 snakes its way down the Schiefe Ebene with train D854, the 12.10 express from Hof to Wurzburg. 18 May 1973. This engine is now preserved at Neuenmarkt-Wirsberg.

Michaeles Stephenson

Above left. A class 41 2-8-2 as originally built between 1936 and 1941 for the Reichsbahn. Three hundred and sixty-six of these fine mixed traffic locomotives were built and No. 41 091 is seen about to leave Kassel on a train of all aluminium coaches to Gottingen. 12 September 1966.   *G. W. Morrison*

Below left. A class 86 2-8-2T hurries a Nuemarkt-Beilngries train alongside the canal near Pollanten.
                          R. J. Manton

Above. The last stronghold of the ubiquitous P8s was the Black Forest area with regular workings between Hausach, Freudenstadt, Boblingen, Tubingen, Horb and Rottweil. No. 038 711-8 was one of the last three survivors of the class and is seen here nearing Alpirsbach on 2 August 1973 with the 16-15 Hausach-Freudenstadt-Horb.
                          J. S. Whiteley

Above left. A Lebach to Saarbrucken train near Walpershofen is hurried along a single line section by Class 23 No. 023 076-3. 22 May 1970.
G. W. Morrison

Below left. An 01[10] rebuilt as an oil burner and renumbered 012 058-4 accelerates an express bound for Munster away from Rheine on 5 April 1971.   *E. Bobrowski*

Above. Class 44 2-10-0 No. 044 487-7 working hard South of Oberkotzau with a freight from Hof to Nurenberg via Marktredwitz.

E. Bobrowski

Above left. 4-6-0 No. 38 3156 heads a Stuttgart-Tuttlingen train just south of Rottweil near the junction with the line to Villingen. 6 June 1968.

L. A. Nixon

Below left. Class 23 2-6-2 No. 023 072-5 climbing away from Gailen-kirchen with the l6.06 Crailsheim - Heilbronn.

Michaeles Stephenson

Above. A 2-10-0 about to enter the depths of the Petersberg tunnel beneath the vineyards at Neef heading a Trier - Koblenz freight. 6 April 1971.

E. Bobrowski

Above. Re-boilered 01 pacific No 001 210-4 built by Krupp in 1937 struggles up the Schiefe Ebene on an appalling wet day in April 1971 with a train bound for Hof.

J. S. Whiteley

Above right. 38 3156 rounds the curve at Talhausen on the 14.58 Horb - Rottweil. 6 June 1968. *L. A. Nixon*

Below right. Reducing line occupation on the single line from Rottweil to Horb are two class 50s, each with tender cab, heading a light freight. 23 May 1970. *G. W. Morrison*

Above. 4-6-0 No. 38 2641 awaits the right away from Marktredwitz with the 11.59 stopping train to Hof on 22 May 1967. *Brian Stephenson*

Above right. Class 65 2-8-4T No. 065 018-4 ambles along the picturesque branch from Aschaffenberg to Miltenberg on a warm April evening in 1971. *J. S. Whiteley*

Below right. A train of empty hoppers behind No. 051 832-4 near Merzig on the line from Trier to Saarbrucken. 22 May 1970. *G. W. Morrison*

Above left. The 14.58 Horb-Rottweil headed by 4-6-0 No. 38 3156 after leaving Eptendorf. 6 June 1968.   *L. A. Nixon*

Below left.   023 037-5 leaving Schwabisch Hall on the 08.05 Heilbronn - Crailsheim on 11 September 1972. The high pitched boiler which cleared the rear coupled axle and also the trailing bogie was a characteristic feature of these 2-6-2s. They were designed for ease of maintenance and had a fairly wide availability having an axle-load of only 17 tons.   *J. S. Whiteley*

Above. 2-6-2T No. 064 094-6 surrounded by class 50s simmers on shed at Tubingen in the early hours of 22 April 1971.   *J. S. Whiteley*

Above. Pacific 012 052-7 waits to set off into the night for Emden from Rheine on an express from Munster.

E. Bobrowski

Above right. Light work for Hof 01 pacific No. 001 202-1 as it leaves Marktschorgast on a Hof-Lichtenfels stopping train. 11 September 1969.

G. W. Morrison

Below right. Two oil burning locomotives of different wheel arrangements pose alongside each other at Rheine. 2-8-2 No. 042 166-9 was designed for mixed traffic work and 2-10-0 No. 043 666-7 for heavy freight.

E. Bobrowski

Above left. Three-cylinder class 39 (Prussian P10) 2-8-2 No. 39 075 working from Junkerath depot, leaves Gerolstein on a wet May morning in 1965 with the 10.19 stopping train for Cologne.

Brian Stephenson

Below left. Re-boilered pacific No. 001 180-9 leaving Falls on 11 May 1973 with train 2850, the 17.29 Hof-Lichtenfels.

J. R. P. Hunt

Above. 01 pacific No. 01 036 as originally built with large smoke-deflectors for the pre-War Deutsche Reichsbahn by Henschel in 1927. This locomotive was one of seventy which were acquired by the post-war Deutsche Reichsbahn after the country was split. It is seen here a few miles inside West Germany leaving Bebra with train D 119, the 10.45 express from Frankfurt to Cottbus in the eastern zone. 20 May 1967.

Brian Stephenson

Above left. A Trier-Saarbrucken train pulls out of Beckingen behind class 23 No. 023 087-0. 22 May 1970.

G. W. Morrison

Below left. Road and rail transport follow closely together down the Neckar Valley. A 2-10-0 is seen near Aistaig on a southbound freight.

J. S. Whiteley

Above. 044 487-7 heading south from Oberkotzau on the Regensberg line with a freight from Hof to Nurenberg.

E. Bobrowski

Above left. A class 38 4-6-0
No. 038 559-1 near Mossigen with
a train from Tubingen to Sig-
maringen. 30 May 1969.

A. G. Orchard

Below left. Class 055 (Prussian G8[1])
0-8-0 No. 055 455-0 halts at Remschied -
Lennep with the L.C.G.B. Ems and
Wupper railtour. 30 April 1972. These
very useful 0-8-0s were built in large
numbers from 1913 onwards.

Brian Stephenson

Above. Hof pacific No. 001 008-2 nears Marktschorgast on the 10.17 Heidelburg-Hof on
13 May 1972. This engine was the first 01 to
enter service in January 1926 being built in Berlin
by Borsig and surprisingly was one of the very
last 01s to remain in service.

J. S. Whiteley

2-10-0 No. 052 425-6 in the woods near Marktschorgast
heading train 2819, the 11.23 stopping train from
Lichtenfels to Hof. 7 May 1973.   *J. S. Whiteley*

Above. An abundance of class 50s at
Saarbrucken shed. *E. Bobrowski*

Right. A birds eye view of a class 78 on shed
at Rottweil. *J. Marsh*

Below. The air brake pump of a class 23.
D. Mills

Above. Class 44 2-10-0 No. 044 463-8 covers Aistaig with a pall of black smoke as it climbs the Neckar valley towards Rottweil. 24 May 1970.
G. W. Morrison

Above right. Class 50 2-10-0's were regular performers on passenger trains working either chimney or tender first. Here No. 053 010-5 nears Etzelwang on the climb from Hartmanshof to Neukirchen on the 17.16 Nurenberg - Amberg just before sunset on 13 May 1972.
J. S. Whiteley

Below right. On a cold December day in 1974 a class 43 is seen leaving Meppen with an ore train from Emden.
D. Mills

Above left. The magnificence of Altenbeken viaduct can be seen in this early morning picture with a 2-10-0 crossing on a mixed freight.   *D. Gouldthorp*

Below left. The signalmen were most obliging at Neuenmarkt-Wirsberg and their box at the south end of the station made a fine vantage point for trains leaving for Bamberg. In this picture taken from the box an un-rebuilt 01 pilots a rebuilt 01 away from the station on The Frankenland, the 13.13 Hof-Saarbrucken 7 May 1973.
J. R. P. Hunt

Above. A not so handsome but very useful class of locomotive, the class 94 (Prussian T 16) 0-10-0T which were built between 1914 and 1924. They were basically heavy shunting locomotives but did in fact handle a certain amount of branch line passenger work. Here No. 094 538-6 leaves Herrnberg on the 14.42 Dillenburg-Gonnern.
J. S. Whiteley

Above left. 044 378-8 leaves a trail of smoke alongside the River Mosel as it slows for Cochem with a train of hoppers. 10 September 1970.

J. S. Whiteley

Below left. Class 23 2-6-2 No. 023 076-3 pulls out of Eiweiler on a Lebach - Saarbrucken local train on 22 May 1970. *G. W. Morrison*

Above. Re-boilered 01 No. 001 200-5 is shrouded in steam as she nears the summit at Marktschorgast heading the 16.47 stopping train from Neuenmarkt - Wirsberg to Hof on a very wet and windy day in April 1971. *J. S. Whiteley*

Above left. Amongst locomotives awaiting their next duties at Tubingen shed in the early hours of 22 April 1971 are a class 64 and two class 50s.

J. S. Whiteley

Below left. A bright morning in the Black Forest sees No. 38 3477 hurrying along between Talhausen and Rottweil heading the 06.05 Horb-Rottweil 28 May 1969.

A. G. Orchard

Above. Many un-rebuilt 01s had the extended running plate at the front cut away for ease of maintenance but No. 001 111-4 is seen here as she was originally constructed in 1934, the only difference being the replacement of the original large smoke-deflectors by the smaller "wing" type which was such a characteristic feature of German locomotives. She is seen here climbing the Schiefe Ebene with an express for Hof.

J. R. P. Hunt

Above. 2-10-0 No. 044 162-6 rolls through Salzbergen with a heavy ore train.   *J. M. Mehltretter*

Above right. A class 50 2-10-0 heads across the Bavarian uplands near Falls with a freight bound for Hof.
                    J. S. Whiteley

Below right. Class 38 4-6-0 No. 038 553-4 heads an attractive rake of six wheeled coaches forming the 09.11 Hausach - Freudenstadt seen nearing Alpirsbach. 22 April 1971.
                    J. S. Whiteley

The conductor of train D146, the 08.13 Dresden-
Munich, hands instructions to the driver of class 01
pacific, No. 01 215 just before departure from Hof
on 21 May 1967.   *Brian Stephenson*